For Stevie, who taught me so much!
C. C.

In memory of Anne Ingram, who offered support
and encouragement from the beginning
M. J.

Text copyright © 2012 by Christopher Cheng
Illustrations copyright © 2012 by Mark Jackson

First U.S. edition 2013

Library of Congress Catalog Card Number 2012942617

ISBN 978-0-7636-6396-4

TLF 17 16 15 14 13 12
10 9 8 7 6 5 4 3 2 1

Printed in Dongguan, Guangdong, China

This book was typeset in Maiandra GD and Kosmik.
The illustrations were done in mixed media.

Candlewick Press
99 Dover Street
Somerville, Massachusetts 02144

visit us at www.candlewick.com

PYTHON

CHRISTOPHER CHENG

ILLUSTRATED BY MARK JACKSON

CANDLEWICK PRESS

It's morning in the bush.
Python stirs and peeks out from her
sheltered resting place.
She warms her head and smells the air
with her forked tongue.
Now it's time to warm her whole body.
She slithers into the open to bask.
A sunny rock is the perfect place.

Pythons, like all reptiles, are ectothermic. That
means they acquire heat from their environment.

Her scales are dull. Her eye scales are cloudy.
Her body has no more room to grow inside her
old scaly covering. It's time to molt.
She rubs her head against a rock, and the old
sack of scales peels back, just like a sock!
Underneath is a shiny snake.
Now her smooth scales glisten in the sun.

Pythons' sleek scales are made of keratin—just like human fingernails. Snakes don't have eyelids, so they can't blink. Their eyes are covered by a single scale.

9

With her body now warm, she glides to the dappled light in the trees. Slowly rippling, she moves along the branches.

A bird drops onto a branch.
He pecks at the bark, unaware that
he's being watched—very, very closely.
Python smells the air, lies in ambush,
and waits.

Pythons flick their tongues in and out to
pick up scents. The snake is not being rude.
She's smelling!

The bird takes another step closer,
focused only on crawling insects.
Python waits no longer.

She misses!

Just in time, the bird flaps away,
safe from razor-sharp teeth.

Pythons have rows of needle-like teeth — perfect for grabbing, hooking, and holding prey, but no good for chewing food.

The sky grows darker.
Python slithers to the bushes
and finds a covered spot. Passing
creatures will not see her here.
She checks the air. The animals of the
night are on the move! A possum scurries
past from her nest in the tree. A bat flaps by,
close to the ground, chasing low-flying moths.
A rat scampers among the grasses. Once more,
Python smells the air, lies in ambush, and waits.

Many pythons have pits just under their lips.
These are sensors that help them detect warm-blooded animals.
Pits are great for hunting in the dark or in shady forests.

15

The rat stops.
He scratches the ground and moves a little closer, looking for seeds to eat.
Python waits no longer.

Dinner!

Pythons are constrictors. A python doesn't
crush its prey; instead, it suffocates it.
(Broken bones would make it harder to eat.)

With a vise-like grip, she holds her prey
tightly and then quickly, carefully,
she coils her body around
her evening feast.

When the rat can no longer breathe,
dinner is ready. Python loosens her coils
and starts to eat, the head first, then the body,
until finally the tail disappears.

Like all snakes, Pythons can unhinge their jaws
and expand their bodies to eat food
that is much bigger than they are.

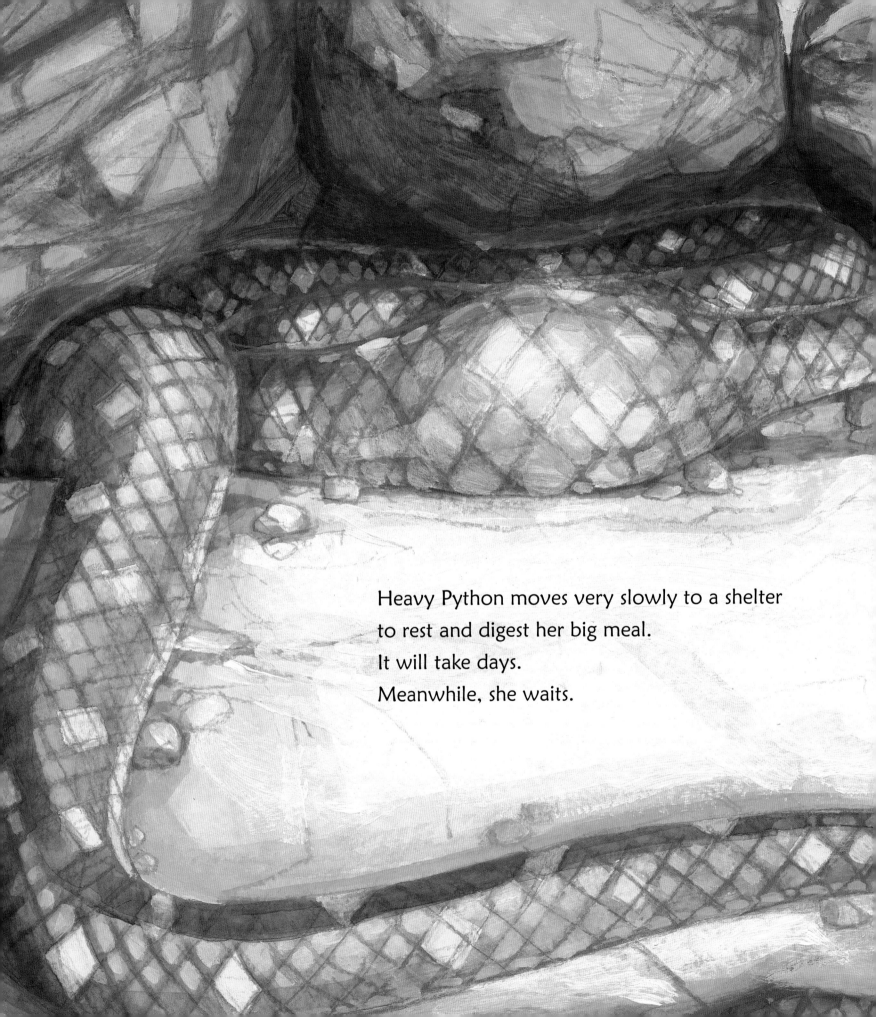

Heavy Python moves very slowly to a shelter
to rest and digest her big meal.
It will take days.
Meanwhile, she waits.

For some pythons, one large meal will be enough to last for weeks and weeks without eating again.

One day Python stays in her nest. She is not alone.
She is coiled around her eggs. Her body shivers,
not from cold, but to help keep her eggs warm.
She leaves her clutch of eggs to warm her body in
the sun, though not for long. She doesn't want her
eggs to cool—or be eaten by a hungry predator!

Some pythons can lay clutches of more than 100 eggs.
The shells are not hard, like birds' eggs. They are softer and leathery.

Quickly, it's back to her nest. And that's where she stays,
for many days and nights, until . . .

An egg is about to hatch. A small slit appears, and out pops a head. Soon many heads are poking out from their shells. The hatchlings smell the air, watch, and wait. Python leaves her clutch to bask in the sun, but this time she doesn't return.

Pythons, like many snakes, are born with an egg tooth to slit the shell. This tooth is soon discarded.

Finally, after many days, the hatchlings leave
their shells. Now they are ready to start their
own lives of smelling, resting, watching . . .

and waiting.

ABOUT PYTHONS

Pythons live in Africa, Asia, and Australia, in steamy tropical rain forests, grasslands, swamps, or stony deserts, and some are wonderful swimmers, too. Pythons are also found in Florida's Everglade National Park. Pythons

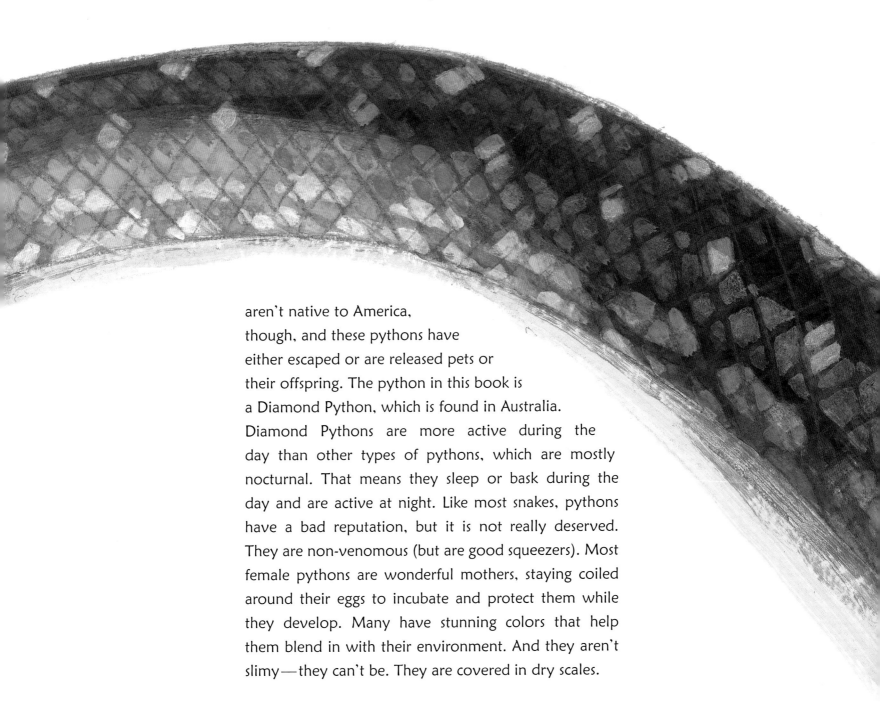

aren't native to America,
though, and these pythons have
either escaped or are released pets or
their offspring. The python in this book is
a Diamond Python, which is found in Australia.
Diamond Pythons are more active during the day than other types of pythons, which are mostly nocturnal. That means they sleep or bask during the day and are active at night. Like most snakes, pythons have a bad reputation, but it is not really deserved. They are non-venomous (but are good squeezers). Most female pythons are wonderful mothers, staying coiled around their eggs to incubate and protect them while they develop. Many have stunning colors that help them blend in with their environment. And they aren't slimy—they can't be. They are covered in dry scales.

INDEX

Look up the pages to find out
about all these python things.

Don't forget to look
at both kinds of word—
this kind and **this kind.**